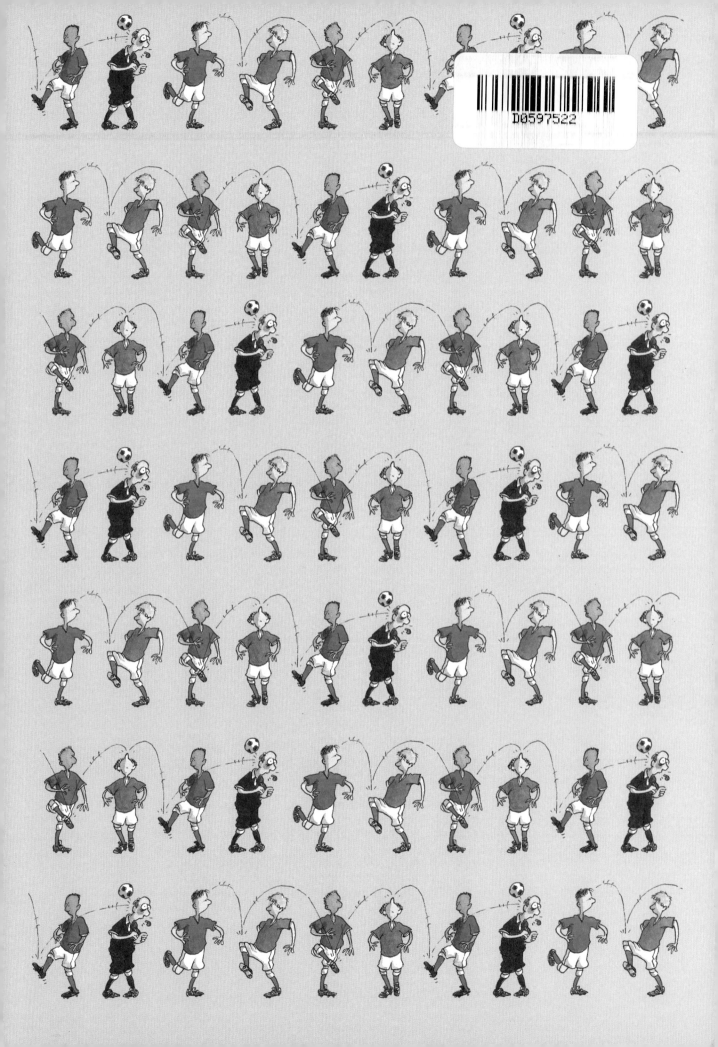

WORLD CUP QUIZ BOOK

MICHAEL COLEMAN

www.michael-coleman.com

Illustrated by
Mike Phillips

■ SCHOLASTIC

Scholastic Children's Books,
Commonwealth House, 1-19 New Oxford Street
London WC1A 1NU, UK

A division of Scholastic Ltd
London ~ New York ~ Toronto ~ Sydney ~ Auckland
Mexico City ~ New Delhi ~ Hong Kong

First published in the UK by Scholastic Ltd, 2002

Text copyright © Michael Coleman, 2002
Illustrations copyright © Mike Phillips, 2002

ISBN 0 439 98105 0

All rights reserved
Typeset by TW Typesetting, Midsomer Norton, Somerset
Printed and bound in Finland by WS Bookwell

2 4 6 8 10 9 7 5 3 1

The right of Michael Coleman and Mike Phillips to be identified as the author and
illustrator of this work respectively has been asserted by them in accordance
with the Copyright, Designs and Patents Act, 1988.

Contents

The World Cup is football's biggest (and sometimes foulest) competition. Why? Quick clue – none of these is the answer...

Because it has the biggest trophy.

Because it's always won by the biggest team.

Because the winners get really big heads.

Either of these could be the answer...

Because it's entered by more countries than any other competition.

No less than 198 countries entered the 2002 World Cup.

Because it's watched by more TV viewers than any other competition.

It's estimated that about half the people on Earth will watch the 2002 finals.

But the most obvious answer is that the World Cup must be football's biggest competition because it needs a big quiz book all to itself – the very book you're holding right now, in fact!

Yes, this is where you'll find the most wicked World Cup questions (and answers). Find out whether your knowledge is world-class or woeful, then use the facts you've discovered to fox your friends and mystify your mates with tasty questions like:

Or under-the-counter questions like:

So if you want to be a wicked World Cup expert, read on. Will you fall foul of the questions in the first round? Or will you fight all the way to the foul final page?

Your very own World Cup competition starts here!

THE WICKED WORLD CUP

Squad squiz

Every country taking part in the World Cup finals is allowed to name a squad of 22 players. So what better way to start a World Cup quiz book than with a squad of 22 general knowledge questions!

1 What did the opening matches in the finals of 1966, 1970, 1974 and 1978 have in common?
a) No goals.
b) The host country didn't win.
c) They were all draws.

2 In 1970, Brazil's Jairzinho scored in every round except the World Cup final. **True or false?**

3 Pierre van Hooijdonk scored four goals in six games for Holland in helping them to qualify for the 1998 finals. What was odd about his performance?
a) He didn't start any of the games.
b) He didn't finish any of the games.

4 The World Cups of 1930 (held in Uruguay), 1934 (Italy), 1966 (England) and 1998 (France) were the only ones to be won by the host country. **True or false?**

8

5 What was peculiar about the 1954 group match between Hungary and South Korea? Were there:
a) More corners than throw-ins.
b) More goals than free kicks.
c) More penalties than kick-offs.

6 In the Mexico finals of 1970, kick-off times were set for the hottest part of the day. **True or false?**

7 What were introduced for the first time in the World Cup finals of 1970?
a) Substitutes.
b) Penalty shoot-outs.
c) Names on shirts.

8 Eight of the Brazil team who won the 1958 final were playing again when Brazil retained the trophy in 1962. **True or false?**

9 Who wore a shirt, tie and jacket for the 1930 World Cup final between Uruguay and Argentina?
a) The referee.
b) The man presenting the trophy.
c) Both team coaches.

10 Argentina's controversial star Diego Maradona once got away with a deliberate handball in a World Cup match against Russia. **True or false?**

11 During a 1982 group match between England and Kuwait, England's Paul Mariner got in trouble after trying to get to a ball that had stuck – where?

a) In one of the goal nets.

b) Under a seat in the Royal Box.

c) Between somebody's feet.

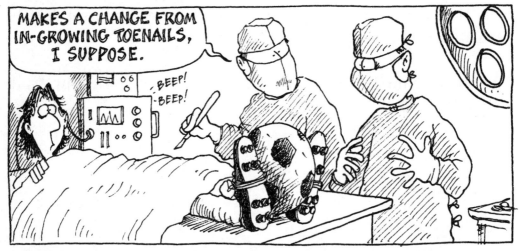

12 Newcastle United star player Jorge Robledo played for England in their 1950 group match against Chile. **True or false?**

13 What did a Portugal player do to England's Bobby Charlton as he ran back to the centre-circle after putting them 2-0 ahead in the 1966 semi-final?

a) Kick his ankle.

b) Shake his hand.

c) Ruffle his hair.

14 England won a trophy at the 1990 World Cup finals. **True or false?**

15 In a qualifying match for the 1998 finals, Guatemala fans pelted United States' goalkeeper Kasey Keller with – what?

a) Bags of 1p's.

b) Bags of peas.

c) Bags of pee.

16 For the first tournament in 1930, the squad of host nation Uruguay all lived in the same hotel. **True or false?**

17 After going 3-0 down against Yugoslavia in a 1974 group match, Zaire's coach substituted – who?
a) His goalkeeper.
b) His captain.
c) His best striker.

18 Jack Kelsey, Wales' goalkeeper in the 1958 finals, used to put glue on his goalkeeping gloves. **True or false?**

19 The famous swerving free kick introduced by Brazil in 1958 was nicknamed – what?
a) The falling leaf.
b) The corkscrew.
c) The banana.

20 When player Renato Gaucho was thrown out of the 1986 Brazil squad because he'd stayed out too late one night, his team-mate Leandro told the coach he didn't want to play either. **True or false?**

21 After the 1970 finals, some newspaper reporters managed to get into the Brazil changing room and insisted on interviewing their star, Pelé...

WHILE HE GOT DRESSED

WHILE HE WAS HAVING A SHOWER

WHILE HE SAT ON THE LOO

22 The mother of Holland's 1974 captain Johan Cruyff was a cleaner at a club named Ajax. **True or false?**

Answers:

1 a), **b)** and **c)** – so you can't have got this one wrong! They all featured the host country and they were all 0-0 draws.

2 False – he scored in the final as well to become the first player to score in every match … seven goals in six games.

3 a) – he scored each of his goals after coming on as a substitute.

4 False – it also happened in West Germany (1974) and Argentina (1978). Will it happen in Japan or Korea in 2002?

5 b) – there were only five free kicks … and Hungary won 9-0!

6 True – the games kicked off at midday because that was the best time for the TV companies who'd paid big money to show the games.

7 a)

8 True – goalkeeper Gilmar, defenders Nilton and Djalma Santos, midfield man Zito and forwards Garrincha, Didì, Vavà and Zagalo.

9 a) – with a pair of knickerbockers (trousers tucked into knee-high socks) to complete the set!

AND THE BEST-DRESSED REFEREE AWARD GOES TO…

FOOTBALL AWARDS

10 True – after scoring against England with a handball in 1986, he used the same method to clear the ball off Argentina's line in a 1990 group match against Russia ... and again the referee didn't spot it. Yes, Maradona was a handy player to have around, all right!

11 c) – between the referee's feet, to be exact. Mariner hauled him out of the way ... and earned a yellow card for it!

12 False – Robledo was Chilean, but was one of the first foreign players to be signed by an English league club.

13 b) – it was a sporting gesture (besides which, nearly bald Charlton had hardly any hair to ruffle!).

14 True – the Fair Play trophy for the team collecting fewest bookings.

15 c) – yuk!

16 False – they all lived in a *house*! But, in the same way as teams today, the squad were supported by sponsors who provided the food ... and furniture!

17 a) – who let in another six goals as Zaire lost 9-0.

18 False – the truth was even stranger; he always used chewing gum.

19 a) – it became known as the banana shot in later years.

20 False – he didn't say anything, just failed to turn up when the squad left.

21 b) – they climbed in fully clothed!

22 True – she persuaded the famous Dutch club to give ten-year-old Cruyff a trial and they signed him on as a schoolboy player.

Famous firsts

As the World Cup is definitely the number one competition in football, here's a quiz about firsts. There's been a World Cup competition held every four years from 1930 except for the years 1942 and 1946 when it was scrapped because of the Second World War.

So – in which years did these "firsts" take place? In case you're not so hot at counting in fours, here are the years:

Answers:

23 1938 – they were The Dutch East Indies (now called Indonesia) … and they played just one match. That year was a straight knockout tournament and after being beaten 6-0 by Hungary, the team went home again. They haven't qualified for the finals since.

24 1958 – in a first round group match between Brazil and England.

25 2002 – shared between Japan and South Korea. Yes, it's always been a single-country affair until now.

26 1962 – the country was Brazil; and they'd probably only have used 11 players if the legendary Pelé hadn't been injured in their second game.

27 1930 – the USA beat both Belgium and Paraguay 3-0 to go through to the semi-finals, where things didn't go quite so yankee-doodle-dandy: they lost 6-1 to Argentina.

28 1974 – Scotland, who won one and drew their other two group games only to miss going through to the next stage on goal difference.

29 1934 – Giampiero Combi of Italy and Frantisek Planicka of Czechoslovakia.

BUTTERFINGERS!

30 1990 – the man who saw red was Pedro Monzon of Argentina. It had taken 52 years and 64 minutes of World Cup finals for it to happen … but just 22 minutes later it happened again as team-mate Gustavo Dezotti was sent off too.

31 1986 – they should have been played in Colombia, but

financial troubles in that country led them to be switched to Mexico for the second time.

32 1982 – Laszlo Kiss, who came on for Hungary after 55 minutes of their group game against El Salvador and scored three goals in ten minutes to help his team win 10-1.

33 1998 – after the numbers of finalists had started at 16 (from 1930–78), then increased to 24 (1982–94).

34 1994 – it was the group game between the USA and Switzerland, which was played in a Detroit stadium ... with a roof.

35 1950 – and then they wished they hadn't, getting knocked out after the first round group matches, which included a 1-0 defeat by the USA.

36 1970 – teams could replace two players from five substitutes.

37 1954 – in glorious black-and-white, of course.

38 1966 – a sneaky one, because everybody (in England, anyway) knows they then went on to win the final at Wembley as well.

39 1978 – it was scored by Rob Rensenbrink of Holland.

Trophy teasers

It's what they're all after – the World Cup
trophy. See if you're a winner by answering
these trophy teasers correctly…

40 There have been two World Cup trophies. What was the first,
officially named in 1950?
a) The Pierre de Coubertin Trophy.
b) The Jules Rimet Trophy.
c) The Henri Delaunay Trophy.

41 Where did this trophy spend the Second World War?

42 What happened to the first trophy?
a) It was stolen and never seen again.
b) It was won outright by one country.
c) It melted.

43 What is the official name of the current trophy?
a) The World Cup – FIFA.
b) The World Cup – UEFA.
c) The World Cup – HAHA.

44 Frenchman Abel Lafleur, in 1930, and Italian Silvio Gazzarriga,
in 1971, both proudly lifted a World Cup trophy – but neither were
footballers. Were they:
a) Sculptors.
b) Guards.
c) Politicians.

Answers:

40 b) – after the Frenchman who had the idea for the competition. (Delaunay had the idea for the European Championships and de Coubertin was responsible for starting the modern Olympic Games. Full of bright ideas, the French!)

41 a) – under the bed of FIFA vice-president, Dr Ottorino Barassi

42 b) – it was presented to Brazil in 1970, in recognition of their third World Cup win. Unfortunately, **a)** and **c)** did happen in 1984; the trophy was stolen and never seen again, with most people thinking that it was melted down and sold.

43 a) – FIFA standing for Fédération Internationale de Football Association (it's French, of course!).

44 a) Lafleur designed the Jules Rimet trophy and Gazzarriga the FIFA World Cup trophy.

CUP COUNTRIES

The great thing about the World Cup is that it gives so many different countries a chance of glory.

Not only are there the superstar countries like Argentina, Brazil, England, Germany and Italy who have won the trophy before, but also a whole alphabet of smaller countries who are never likely to, from Albania to Zimbabwe.

Big or small, each country in the world has a fact-filled footballing history. There are glorious facts, funny facts, quirky facts and facts that they'd prefer to forget about if they could. Facts like these, in fact…

The country collection

Match these (not always complimentary) facts to this list of countries:

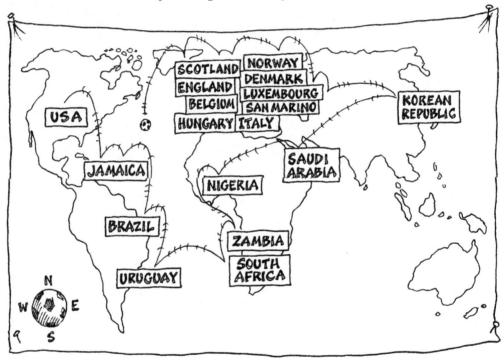

45 Their first "international" match took place in 1914 – against English club side Exeter City.

46 Their triumphant 1934 team included Argentinian players – but they didn't call themselves Argentina.

47 They may have played in the first World Cup finals in 1930, but it took them another 40 years to win a match.

48 Their nickname is "The Reggae Boyz".

49 When they beat Switzerland 2-1 in a qualifier in 1982, they celebrated their goals with a traditional stiff upper lip!

50 Their goalkeeper also drove the team coach!

51 They were the first African country to win the Olympic football gold medal in 1996.

52 They lost their first international 11-3 to Sweden.

53 They've never finished higher than bottom in every World Cup qualifying group they've been in!

54 Their first international was against Cameroon in 1992.

55 Their footballers weren't allowed to be paid for playing internationals until 1976.

56 They've gone to the World Cup finals eight times, but never yet reached the second round.

57 World Cup 2002 joint hosts, they played their first international at the 1948 Olympic Games.

58 A survey showed that almost half the population of their country didn't know they had a team playing in the 1998 World Cup finals!

59 Their victorious defence in 1930 was nicknamed "The Iron Curtain".

60 Their nickname is "The Desert Warriors".

61 They lost almost their entire squad in a plane crash while travelling to a 1993 qualifying game in Senegal.

62 Out of 51 international matches played between June 1950 and November 1955 they lost just once.

Answers:

45 Brazil – they won 2-0!

46 Italy – in 1934 you could play for Italy if you had Italian ancestors.

47 Belgium – who took part in 1930 but didn't win a finals game until 1970.

48 Jamaica

49 England – they were following the advice of Sir Harold Thompson, Chairman of the FA, who'd said English players should set a good example and not go around kissing each other after scoring a goal!

50 San Marino – because all their players were part-time and his other job was as a travel agent.

51 Nigeria

52 Norway

53 Luxembourg

54 South Africa – until then they'd been barred from international football because of their government's policy of keeping different races separate. There were even different football leagues for people with different coloured skins!

55 Denmark
56 Scotland
57 Korean Republic (then South Korea) – they beat Mexico 5-3.
58 USA – maybe it was just as well: they lost all three of their group games.
59 Uruguay
60 Saudi Arabia
61 Zambia – the only four squad players to survive played for European clubs and were travelling to the match on a different plane.
62 Hungary

Shuffling shirts

From the yellow of Brazil to the blue of Italy, the stripes of Argentina to the chessboard design of Croatia, the World Cup is a football shirt showcase.

Here are three short shirt quizzes to test your shirt-term memory. In each of them, one of the statements is false, but the others are true. See if you can you sort out the facts from the fiction by spotting the odd one out.

French farces
63 In the 1978 finals, France and Hungary couldn't start their match because they'd both brought the same colour shirts.
64 France had so little confidence in 1958 that they only took enough shirts to the finals in Sweden for the first round matches.
65 In 1930, France's footballers played in shirts borrowed from the French rugby team.
66 When they started their triumphant 1998 World Cup campaign some of the French players were told to wear shirts that were the wrong size.

Answers:
63 True
64 True – just three sets; France quickly had to get some more as they went on to reach the semi-finals.
65 False
66 True – why? Because the shirts had been made before the squad was picked!

Colour concerns

67 Italy are known as "The Azzurri" because they wear blue shirts.

68 Argentina began to wear striped shirts after their first captain revealed that he was colour-blind and couldn't distinguish between plain colours.

69 In 1998, TV commentators complained about Croatia because they couldn't see the numbers on their shirts.

70 Brazil changed the colour of their shirts from white to yellow because they were so disappointed at not winning the World Cup one year.

Answers:

67 True – because *azzuri* is Italian for "blues".

68 False

69 True – they said they couldn't read the black numbers on their red-and-white squared shirts.

I DON'T CARE WHAT THE COMMENTATORS SAY, I FEEL RIDICULOUS IN THIS!

70 True – it happened in 1950 and they changed their white shorts to the famous blue while they were at it.

Shirt tales

71 In 1998, Michael Owen of England had a shirt number higher than his age. **True or false?**

72 Carlos Babington was so pleased to be picked for his country in 1974 that he wore his Argentina shirt in bed. **True or false?**

73 Brazil's manager in 1970, Mario Zagalo, said that every player in his team had to have three shirts. **True or false?**

74 In 2001, after he'd scored a hat trick in England's 5-1 qualifying match defeat of Germany, Michael Owen left the field wearing a green Germany shirt. **True or false?**

Answers:

71 True – Owen was aged 18 and his shirt number was 20.

72 True

73 False – Zagalo said they should have *two* shirts. It was his way of explaining how he expected all his players to both attack and defend. It worked, too: Brazil won the World Cup that year.

74 True. He was wearing a German shirt he'd swapped for his own. He then had to go into the Germans' changing room and beg for his England shirt back again to keep as a souvenir for himself!

Questionable qualification

Although only 32 countries can win their way through to reach the finals of the World Cup, just about every country in the world takes part in the qualifying competition.

Question:

75 Sometimes a country will enter even though life is made difficult for them. In 1958, for instance, the Northern Ireland team had to break one of their own laws in order to play in the finals. What did the law say?

a) Competing against certain countries was illegal.

b) Playing football on a Sunday was illegal.

c) Taking sports equipment out of the country was illegal.

Answer:
75 b) The team ignored the law, went ahead with their games – and nobody arrested them. Mind you, they did really well and reached the quarter-finals. Maybe it would have been different if they'd been badly beaten!

Coming – or going?

For the qualifying matches, countries in the same part of the world are put into groups and play each other in mini-leagues to decide which of them will qualify for the finals…

Question:

76 Host countries don't have to qualify. As joint hosts in 2002, Japan and South Korea are guaranteed two of the 32 places in the finals. So how many qualifying places are there to play for?

Answer:
76 29. The World Cup holders (in this case France, from 1998) don't have to qualify for the next competition either.

Qualifying matches have been known to produce some unbelievable scenes. How unbelievable? Stretch your imagination in this quiz...

77 In 1954, Turkey and Spain made up a two-country group. Turkey qualified – but not by beating Spain on the pitch. How did they do it?
a) The teams tossed up and Turkey won.
b) Spain were disqualified after a pitch invasion by their fans.
c) Turkey were awarded the tie after Spain turned up late.

78 Italy and Northern Ireland were battling for top place in their 1958 group. Italy only had to draw to qualify. But although the match ended 2-2, Northern Ireland still went through. How?
a) Northern Ireland were awarded a bonus place for good sportsmanship.
b) Italy were disqualified for trying to bribe the referee.
c) The match had to be replayed and Northern Ireland won it.

79 In 1978, Tunisia became the first country to qualify for the finals by means of ... what?
a) A golden goal in extra-time.
b) A penalty shoot-out.
c) Scoring more away goals.

HELLO, WE'RE THE WELSH TEAM

IS THAT AFRICAN WELSH, OR ASIAN WELSH?

80 Most people know that Wales is a European country, but in 1958 they were declared winners of the Africa and Asia group. How come?
a) A secretary wrongly typed their name on to a results sheet.
b) They were added to a group of one, which they won.
c) The real winners of the group dropped out and they took their place.

81 In 1974 Belgium only managed second place in their qualifying group even though they hadn't – what?
a) Conceded a goal.
b) Lost a match.
c) Played against a team that finished with 11 men.

82 The opening qualifying game of the 1998 World Cup took place on a grass pitch which the groundsman claimed he kept in trim by using … what?

83 In 1970, El Salvador and Honduras had to play each other three times in qualifying matches. They were so enthusiastically supported that the games were followed by another contest between the two countries. Was it a…
a) War.
b) Boxing tournament.
c) Song contest.

84 Scotland kicked off their 1998 qualifying match against Estonia – without somebody on the pitch. Who?
a) The referee.
b) One of Scotland's players.
c) An Estonian player.

85 Italian and English TV companies decided not to broadcast the 1978 qualifying group match between Italy and England. Why not?
a) They were worried too many fans would watch.
b) They thought it would be a rotten game.
c) They didn't want to be blamed if their team lost the match.

Answers:

77 a) – after a drawn match they tossed up ... and Turkey won the toss.

78 c) – with quite a few group games still to come, Italy refused to accept the result of the drawn match because it had been played with a reserve referee in charge. If they'd known a draw would have been good enough, they'd have accepted it! As it was, when the game was replayed Northern Ireland won 2-1 and went through.

79 b) – and it was third time lucky for Tunisia against close rivals Morocco. Twice before the two countries had been made to decide their group by tossing a coin ... and Tunisia had lost both times!

80 c) Israel were left alone in their Africa/Asia group when all the other teams refused to play them. FIFA held a draw for second-placed teams in other groups for a play-off game. Wales won the draw – and the match against Israel.

81 a) and **b)** – they were beaten into second place by Holland, against whom they'd twice drawn 0-0: unluckily for them, Holland had done better against the other teams in the group and Belgium lost out on goal difference.

82 b) it was the pitch in the tiny 4,000-capacity ground Dominica used for their match against Antigua.

83 a) – the matches actually got both countries so worked up that a short war broke out between them!

84 c) more correctly, without a *single* Estonian player! They didn't turn up, in protest at the game being suddenly moved from an evening kick-off to an afternoon. The game was abandoned and eventually replayed five months later.

85 a) – it was an afternoon match and TV companies in both countries wouldn't show the game in case they caused a mass skiving off from work (and school!).

We're not playing with you!

Nowadays virtually every country on Earth takes part in the World Cup but it's been known for countries to decide that they're not going to take part. All sorts of reasons have been offered but, believe it or not, it's often simply because the country is sulking!

Here's a collection of World Cup withdrawals – was there a serious reason or were they simply sulking sides?

86 Although they were to become world champions in 1934 and 1938, Italy didn't take part in the first finals in Uruguay in 1930. **Serious or sulking?**

87 Uruguay, the reigning champions after their victory in 1930, didn't take part in the 1934 competition in Italy. **Serious or sulking?**

88 In 1974 the USSR pulled out because they didn't want to play a deciding match against Chile. **Serious or sulking?**

89 India didn't take part in the 1950 World Cup finals either. **Serious or sulking?**

90 Austria didn't take part in the 1938 finals in France. **Serious or sulking?**

91 France withdrew from the 1950 finals in Brazil. **Serious or sulking?**

92 Scotland didn't go to the 1950 finals in Brazil, even though they'd qualified. **Serious or sulking?**

93 After being host country in 1986, Mexico didn't take part in the 1990 finals in Italy. **Serious or sulking?**

Answers:

86 Sulking! Italy had wanted to be the host country. When Uruguay was chosen they stayed at home instead.

87 Sulking! To pay back the European team for not visiting them, Uruguay refused to visit Europe.

88 Serious. They were protesting because the stadium they were due to play in had once been used as a prison.

89 Sulking! They wanted to play in bare feet and the rules didn't allow it – so they withdrew before they were kicked out!

90 Serious. Germany had made one of the moves which led to the Second World War and invaded Austria. (All the best Austrian players became "Germans". One of them – Hans Pesser – ended up sulking too. When Germany were knocked out by Switzerland he got sent off!)

91 Serious. They'd been told their group games would be at grounds which were 2,000 miles apart. In the days before fast air-travel that meant a really loooooonnnggg journey.

92 Sulking! The British Championship (an annual league competition between England, Northern Ireland, Scotland and

---

Wales) had been made into its own little qualifying group, with both the winners and runners-up being awarded places in the finals. Scotland said they wouldn't go if they only came second. They did, so they didn't.

93 Serious. The World Cup organizing body, FIFA, had banned Mexico as a punishment for putting over-age players into its team for the World Under-20's Cup.

PERFECT HOSTS

Mixed-up hosts

The country in which the World Cup finals are played is called the host country. Nowadays it's chosen five or six years before the event – from a *host* of applicants!

Discover the names of the host countries in these statements. All the letters are supplied but they've been scrambled up!

94 The only two-time hosts to date have been REFCAN and ECOMIX.
95 ... But in 2006, REGMYNA will join them as they host the World Cup for the second time.
96 When H LICE hosted the World Cup, all the schools were closed while the matches were on!

IF ONLY THEY'D HOLD THE WORLD CUP **EVERY** YEAR

EVERY MONTH WOULD BE NICE

97 WESNED were the hosts the year that Brazil became the only country so far to win the World Cup outside their own continent.
98 To date, the only host not in Europe and South America has been TED IS TEA NUTS.
99 N DANGLE was the happy host of the 1966 finals!
100 The year A RAIN GENT both hosted and won the World Cup, Juventus manager Giovanni Trapatonni said unkindly, "If the competition had been held anywhere else they wouldn't even have survived the first round."

Answers:

94 FRANCE (in 1938 and 1998) and MEXICO (in 1970 and 1986) have been hosts twice.

95 GERMANY were hosts in 1974 and have been chosen again for 2006.

96 CHILE made their students smile in 1962. (Governments everywhere, are you reading this!)

97 SWEDEN – who reached the World Cup final themselves.

98 UNITED STATES, in 1994.

99 ENGLAND.

100 ARGENTINA, in 1978.

Stadium stumpers

Host countries usually set about improving their existing stadiums or, quite often, building brand new stadiums for the tournament – as France did for the 1998 World Cup. They then had the problem of deciding what to call it. Their first idea was to name the stadium after their most famous player, Michel Platini.

101 Easy question: What did Platini say, "Oui" or "Non"?

101 Easy answer: Non. So the place was named, rather less interestingly, *The Stade de France* (The Stadium of France).

Sometimes this can cause a problem. For the first ever finals in 1930, Uruguay desperately wanted to play their opening match in the wonderful new Centenary Stadium they'd had especially built. There was only problem – it wasn't ready!

102 What happened?

a) Uruguay played the opening match somewhere else.

b) Uruguay used the unfinished stadium, with fans sitting on boxes.

c) Uruguay arranged for their opening match to be delayed.

> **Answer:**
> **102 c)** Five days after the tournament started, with the Centenary Stadium now finished, Uruguay played their opening match.

See how you get on with these stadium stumpers…

Odd grounds out

Unlike Michel Platini, football people don't always refuse permission for football grounds to be named after them. (If they're dead, they can't refuse!) Here's a selection of grounds which have seen World Cup final matches. Which were named after footballers, and which weren't?

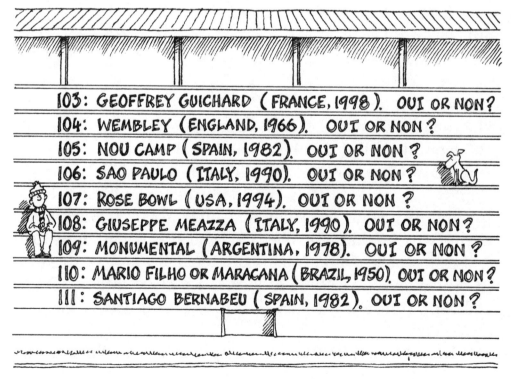

103: GEOFFREY GUICHARD (FRANCE, 1998). OUI OR NON?

104: WEMBLEY (ENGLAND, 1966). OUI OR NON?

105: NOU CAMP (SPAIN, 1982). OUI OR NON?

106: SAO PAULO (ITALY, 1990). OUI OR NON?

107: ROSE BOWL (USA, 1994). OUI OR NON?

108: GIUSEPPE MEAZZA (ITALY, 1990). OUI OR NON?

109: MONUMENTAL (ARGENTINA, 1978). OUI OR NON?

110: MARIO FILHO OR MARACANA (BRAZIL, 1950). OUI OR NON?

111: SANTIAGO BERNABEU (SPAIN, 1982). OUI OR NON?

Answers:

Actually, just ONE of the grounds was named after a footballer. Here's the full list.

103 Non. Geoffrey Guichard was a local grocer. He founded the French club St Etienne whose home ground it is (and at which Scotland played one of their group games in the 1998 finals).

104 Non. Wembley was named after the area of West London, Wembley Park, where it was built. Bor-ing!

105 Non. Bor-ing again, this time in Spanish. *Nou Camp* simply means *New Ground*!

106 Non. *Sao Paulo* means *St Paul* and although the disciple was definitely a real person there's no evidence that he ever played football!

107 Non. It's called that because of its shape.

108 OUI!! Giuseppe Meazza played in both of Italy's World Cup winning sides in 1934 and 1938. The ground is also home to top Italian clubs AC Milan and Inter Milan. It was known as the San Siro (like Wembley, after the area it's in) until 1979 and then renamed after Milan-born Meazza who was a star for AC Milan and Inter Milan as well as for his country.

109 Non. It means the same in Spanish as it does in English – very big!

110 Non. Mario Filho was the mayor of Rio de Janeiro who saw the building of the stadium through to completion. It's better known as The Maracana stadium – but Maracana wasn't a footballer either. It's the name of a muddy river that flows nearby!

111 Non. The stadium is home to Spanish club Real Madrid and named after the club's longest-serving president.

Grounds for a decision

Decisions have to be taken about the insides of grounds as well as the outsides. If you were the host nation, what would you decide to do in the following scenarios…?

112 You're in Montevideo, Uruguay in 1930 and you want to name one of the three stands in the newly-built Centenary Stadium in a way that shows you expect Uruguay to win the World Cup that year. The other two stands are called *Colombes* and *Amsterdam*. What do you call the third?
a) Montevideo.
b) Uruguay.
c) Centenario.

113 You have to decide what colour to paint the seats in Brazil's massive *Maracana Stadium*. What do you go for?
a) Fiery red, to encourage the fans to cheer more wildly.
b) Dark grey, so that the fans won't be able to see they're dirty.
c) Pale blue, to keep the fans calm.

I'M THINKING SPLASHES OF FIERY RED WITH DABS OF PALE BLUE, WHAT D'YOU SAY?

GREY!

114 Still in the Maracana, you now want to name the two changing rooms after two famous Brazilians. Who do you choose?

(a) US, US, US! TWO FAMOUS POLITICIANS (b) US, US, US! TWO FAMOUS SINGERS (c) US, US, US! TWO FAMOUS FOOTBALLERS

Answers:

112 a) – the two other stands were named *Colombes* and *Amsterdam* because they were the cities in which Uruguay had won the Olympic football title in 1924 and 1928. Calling the third stand *Montevideo* meant they expected to complete a set of three titles!

113 c) – and with a capacity of 200,000 that meant a lot of blue seats!

114 c) – the home changing room is named after Pelé, star of Brazil's 1958 and 1970 winning teams, and the away changing room after Garrincha, star of the 1958 and 1962 teams.

FRANTIC FANS AND MAD MEDIA

Thanks to the media, the World Cup isn't only followed by fans at the matches but by readers, viewers and listeners in every corner of the world – and they all get really excited!

During the 1998 finals, up to 15,000 Brazilian fans would queue from five o'clock in the morning to watch their team – and that was just to see them do their training!

IS THIS THE QUEUE FOR THE TRAINING SESSION?

NO, WE'RE WAITING TO SEE THE BOOTS BEING CLEANED

Question:

115 When the 2002 World Cup takes place in Japan and South Korea you're bound to see players doing what players do at the end of matches nowadays – applauding the fans who have come to watch them play. Well, apart from the players of one team. You won't see Japanese players applauding their fans. What will they do instead?

a) Bow to them.

b) Run over and shake some of their hands.

c) Ignore them.

> **Answer:**
> **115 a)** – bowing is the nice, traditional Japanese greeting.

Strange supporters

Excited supporters can do the strangest things. Find out exactly how strange in this collection of fantastic World Cup fan-aticism!

116 Japan's supporters would carry little bags into the ground whenever they watched a match during the 1998 finals. What was in them?

a) Nothing.

b) Sweets to throw to the Japanese players.

c) Rubbish.

117 In 1994 about 20 American fans left the ground when Switzerland scored in the opening match of the 1994 finals. Why?
a) They thought the game had finished.
b) They thought America were going to lose badly and couldn't bear to watch.
c) They were protesting about the Swiss fans' loud cheering.

118 In 1958 a group of singing Swedish fans were banned from the World Cup final between Sweden and Brazil. Why?
a) They were singing rude Swedish songs.
b) They were singing so loudly the players couldn't hear the referee's whistle.
c) They weren't making the Brazilian fans happy.

119 During the 1998 World Cup a large group of students in Bangladesh poured out into the streets to protest. What about?
a) Too few World Cup matches on TV.
b) Not having enough time to watch the matches on TV.
c) The price of TVs.

120 In 1994, a few Republic of Ireland fans actually had a pee while they watched their team play. Were they...
a) In a packed ground and unable to get out to the loo.
b) Preparing very unpleasant bombs to throw at opposing players.
c) Standing in a loo with a view of the match.

Answers:

116 a) – but they're full when they come out. The Japanese fans carry little bags (in their team's colours!) so that they can clear up their rubbish and take it home again. (Japan's players are equally tidy, often leaving their changing room cleaner than it was when they arrived!)

117 a) – the American fans were simply confused. They thought a soccer match ended when a goal was scored!

118 c) – they were cheerleaders who were encouraging the Swedish fans to shout for their team. The FIFA organizers didn't think this was fair in a final so the cheerleaders were banned (and without them Sweden lost 2-5 to Brazil).

119 b) – the reason the students didn't have enough watching time was because they were in the middle of their exams. Their protest was aimed at having their exams postponed so that they could watch the football!

120 c) – a Dublin hotel installed TV sets in their loos so that resident fans could see and pee at the same time!

Mad media

There can't be many people on Earth who don't know when the World Cup is being played. The newspapers go nuts, radios rave and TVs trumpet with every little detail of what's happening.

Try not to go raving mad yourself with these questions on the media...

121 During the 1990 finals in Italy, Argentina's star Diego Maradona won a vote organized by an Italian newspaper. What was it for?
a) Most hated man.
b) Fattest footballer.
c) Best player in the world.

I'D LIKE TO THANK MY LOCAL BAKERS, THE STAFF AT HAPPY HAMBURGER...

122 England striker Jimmy Greaves, playing against Brazil in the 1962 quarter-finals, managed to capture a stray dog which ran on to the pitch. What comment did the English newspapers make about the incident?
a) Greaves showed the dog what nippy footwork was all about.
b) The dog showed Greaves how to make a biting tackle.
c) Capturing the dog was the best thing Greaves did in the tournament.

123 What was the title of Scotland's song for the 1974 finals in West Germany?
a) *Easy, Easy*
b) *Highs and Lows*
c) *Brave Boys*

124 The music industry doesn't miss out at World Cup time, either. What was the title of England's hit song for the Mexico finals in 1970?
a) *Viva Football*
b) *Back Home*
c) *Hit The High Spots*

125 At the start of April 1998, a radio station in Portugal was the first to break some good news to listeners still trying to recover from the fact that Portugal hadn't qualified for the finals in France. What was it?
a) Portugal had been such unlucky losers they weren't going to have to qualify for the 2002 finals.
b) Iran had dropped out of the 1998 finals and Portugal was taking its place.
c) Portugal had been chosen as the host country for the 2012 finals.

126 Nowadays the finals have an official film made about them. What was the film of the 1986 finals in Argentina called?
a) *Glory*
b) *Champion*
c) *Hero*

127 Last but nowhere near least: television. TV coverage of the 1994 World Cup always had plenty of shots of the bare arms and legs of the sun-tanned spectators in the crowd. But the government of Iran thought this wasn't decent. What did they show instead?
a) Crowd shots of spectators in fur coats.
b) Advertisements for ankle-length dresses.
c) A blank screen.

128 Because the World Cup has so many viewers, companies pay good money to advertise themselves in any way they can. In 1978, for instance, one sports equipment company paid the French team to wear their football boots. The players didn't think they were paying enough, though. What did they do?

a) Wore boots made by another company.

b) Painted their boots black.

c) Took their boots off in the middle of a match.

129 Sponsors also pay loads of money to have their names on the front of football shirts so that they'll be seen all game by TV viewers. Germany and England, semi-final rivals in 1990, both had sponsors. Who were they?

Germany:

a) A drink producer.

b) A car maker.

c) A credit card company.

England:

a) A food company.

b) A car breakdown company.

c) A bank.

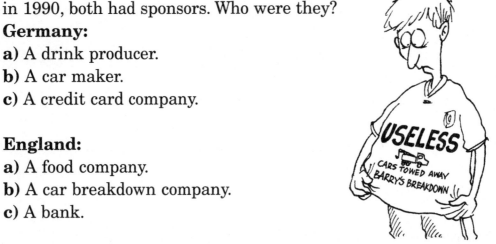

130 Fans usually watch players on TV, but for the Romanian team in 1998 things worked the other way round: the players watched the fans on TV. What were the fans doing?

a) Celebrating Romanian goals being scored.

b) Demonstrating how they wanted Romanian goals to be scored.

c) Praying for Romanian goals to be scored.

131 In all areas of the media ex-players are employed to use their knowledge of the game to point the ignorant public in the right direction. Ex-England star Kevin Keegan was in this position when Romania played England in a 1998 group match. What was his analysis of the situation with the teams at 1-1 and not long to go?

a) "I've got a feeling Romania might score a late winner."

b) "Anybody can see the teams have decided to settle for a draw."

c) "There's only one team going to win this – England."

Answers:

121 a) – Maradona was playing for Argentina when they beat hosts Italy on penalties in the semi-final. That was bad enough, but it happened at the ground of Napoli ... the Italian club Maradona played for!

122 c) – showing yet again how difficult it is to muzzle the press!

123 a)

124 b)

WE WERE KNOCKED OUT SO EASY, EASY— WE'RE DREADING GOING BACK HOME!

125 b) – it happened at the very start of April ... on the 1st, in fact. Yes, it was an April Fool's joke.

126 c) – in honour of Diego Maradona, who'd played brilliantly for Argentina even though he'd punched one goal in against England. Maybe that's why the film-makers thought he'd won the World Cup single-handed!

127 a) – they inserted shots of one of their own fully-dressed football crowds, then switched back to the actual match. Trouble was, their shots had been taken on an overcast day and the match was being played in blazing sunshine...

128 b) – they still wore the boots, but painted over the company's famous white stripes so that viewers couldn't see them.

JUST THE BOOTS, PIERRE!

WHAT?

129 Germany b) – a quality car manufacturer.
England b) – a breakdown recovery company.

Is it any wonder that when the semi-final went to a penalty shoot-out, Germany won it? England's defence broke down!
130 a) – to inspire his players before their group match against England, the Romanian coach asked to be sent TV footage of the fans at home celebrating the goals Romania had scored in their previous match against Colombia. It worked – duly inspired, Romania beat England 2-1 with a goal in the last minute!
131 c) – whereupon Romania promptly scored a last-minute goal to win the game 2-1!

WORLD CUP COACHES

Every team in the World Cup has somebody in charge. He used to be called a manager but nowadays he's called the head coach. If his team does badly, he's called a lot more than that!

Scotland didn't do very well in 1978, and their manager Ally McLeod felt so miserable that when a dog approached him in the street he told it, "You are my only friend in the world!" He was wrong: it promptly bit him!

Some players don't think they need a coach. In 1950, England's world-famous forward Stanley Matthews said that players good enough to be internationals should be left alone to play their own game and not told how to do it by a manager. Maybe that was why they then lost 0-1 to the USA.

On the other hand, some coaches definitely need to leave the players alone ... like Bora Milutinovic, for instance. To date he's already been to four successive World Cup finals as coach of four different teams: Mexico in 1986, Costa Rica in 1990, USA in 1994 and Nigeria in 1998. What you might call a coach tour!

I'll manage!

See if you can manage to sort out the facts from the fantasies in this selection of statements about World Cup coaches.

132 One of Saudi Arabia's coaches, Leo Beenhakker, was sacked for arguing with a Prince. **True or false?**

133 The Romanian team for the 1930 World Cup was picked by their Queen Carol. **True or false?**

134 In 1996 Mario Kempes (a World Cup winner with Argentina in 1978) was appointed coach of Albania. He was only paid £10 a week, even though the average salary in Albania was £100,000 a year. **True or false?**

135 Graham Taylor, manager of the England team for the 1994 World Cup campaign, described being manager as "the important job". **True or false?**

136 When 1998 finalists Iran and Jamaica played a friendly, Iran tried to stop Jamaica's trainer attending the match – because she was a woman. **True or false?**

137 Before flying out to a friendly match, some of England's 1966 squad disobeyed their manager's orders and went out for a drink. When they returned it was to find that they'd been locked out of their hotel. **True or false?**

138 Vittorio Pozzo, Italy's winning manager in 1934 and 1938, could walk on water. **True or false?**

139 Gérard Houllier, currently manager of Liverpool, picked up a World Cup winners' medal in 1978. **True or false?**

Answers:

132 True – the coach hadn't wanted to obey enthusiastic Prince Faisal's order to substitute one of his players during a match. Maybe this helps explain how Saudi Arabia managed to get through eight different coaches on their way to the 1998 finals!

133 False – Carol was their king, but he did pick the squad. He also arranged for the players to have time off from work!

134 False – it was the other way round: Kempes was said to have been paid £100,000 while the average salary in Albania was £10 per week.

135 False – Taylor said managing England was "the *impossible* job". Maybe that's why England failed to qualify for the 1994 finals.

136 True – women aren't allowed to go to football matches in Iran.

137 False – the players found their passports on their beds as a warning.

138 True – kind of. After Italy had won the 1938 final, Pozzo was so overwhelmed that he didn't realize water from a bucket was pouring into his shoes. By the time he did, they were soaked – so he had to walk on the water!

139 False – but he did pick one up in 1998. As Technical Director to the French team, Houllier was awarded an honorary medal for helping France to victory.

Coach's quotes

Coaches are often called on for a few words of wisdom – and nearly as often reply with lots of words of rubbish!

Some words in these coach's quotes have been replaced by RUBBISH; work out what they really said!

Just in case you're rubbish at this sort of quiz, here are the words you're looking for:

ATMOSPHERE; CHANCE; DOGS; ELEVEN; WALK; GOOD; GOBI DESERT; MEDITERRANEAN; NOTHING

140 Jack Charlton of the Republic of Ireland complaining in 1994 about the heat in Florida:

> *We're from Ireland, not the RUBBISH.*

141 Dr Deitz of Hungary in 1938:

> *If we lose to Switzerland I shall RUBBISH home.*

142 Maturana of Colombia after being beaten by USA in 1994:

> *It's a shame the law allows only two substitutions. Otherwise I would have replaced all RUBBISH players.*

143 Sir Alf Ramsey took his England team to the World Cup in 1970 saying:

> *We have RUBBISH to learn from the Brazilians.*

144 Jupp Derwall of Germany before their match against Algeria in 1982:

> *If we lose the players should be thrown into the RUBBISH.*

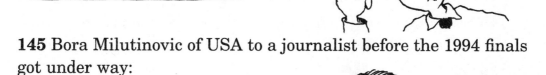

145 Bora Milutinovic of USA to a journalist before the 1994 finals got under way:

> *I do not like for me or my players to be called RUBBISH.*

146 Clemens Westerhof of Nigeria, after his team played in front of a big crowd against Argentina in 1994:

> *Any player not inspired by that RUBBISH should go and play golf with his grandmother.*

147 Bobby Robson of England said when his team began the 1990 finals badly:

> *Maybe we're not as RUBBISH as we thought we were.*

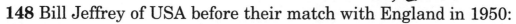

148 Bill Jeffrey of USA before their match with England in 1950:

> *We have no RUBBISH.*

Answers:

140 *We're from Ireland, not the <u>Gobi Desert</u>.*

141 *If we lose to Switzerland I shall <u>walk</u> home.* Fortunately for Dr Deitz's feet, Hungary won 2-0.

142 *It's a shame the law allows only two substitutions. Otherwise I would have replaced all <u>eleven</u> players.*

143 *We have <u>nothing</u> to learn from the Brazilians.* Except how to win the 1970 World Cup, which is what Brazil did!

144 *If we lose the players should be thrown into the <u>Mediterranean</u>.* They did lose, 1-2, in one of the biggest World Cup shocks ever – but the players stayed on dry land and fought their way to the final where they lost to Italy.

145 *I do not like for me or my players to be called <u>dogs</u>.* The coach was from Serbia and had misunderstood. He'd thought they were being insulted, but the journalist had only asked how he felt about his team being *under*dogs!

146 *Any player not inspired by that <u>atmosphere</u> should go and play golf with his grandmother.*

147 *Maybe we're not as <u>good</u> as we thought we were.* In the event, England weren't as rubbish as everybody else thought they were – they reached the semi-finals.

148 *We have no <u>chance</u>,* said Jeffrey. His USA team promptly went out and won 1-0.

Crafty coaching

Coaches have the job of working out tactics, but once their players are out on the pitch anything can happen.

At the start of their 1978 final against Holland, for instance, Argentina planned a sneaky tactic in advance. They complained to the referee about a plaster cast one of the Dutch players had on his arm. Their hope was that it would put the Dutch off, or maybe even force the referee to say that the player couldn't take part in the game. What they didn't expect was that the Dutch would immediately come up with a tactic of their own – threatening to walk off the pitch and leave Argentina to play themselves!

What sort of crafty coach would you be? Crack the clues and discover the world-class tactics that were used in this World Cup collection:

149 Chile's coach for the 1998 finals, Xavier Askargorta, encouraged his players not to wear – what? (Clue: what he said wasn't what his players wanted to 'ear!)

150 Argentina's 1986 coach Carlos Bilardo thought it was essential that, before every game, he did – what? (Clue: it improved his smile, anyway.)

151 Romania's secret weapon in 1998 was something in their diet called telemea. What was it? (Clue: the squad believed it turned them from mice into men!)

152 Farooq Aziz was selected by his country, Pakistan, for a 1994 qualifying match against China. As an amateur, though, some tactics had to be used so that he could get two weeks' extra holiday from – where? (Clue: he had to make up for it at home.)

153 Italy's 1934 champions were spurred into action by threats of – what? (Clue: they knew if they didn't battle hard they'd be battling even harder.)

154 The USA team prepared for their famous 1950 victory over England by doing – what? (Clue: the tactic gave England a rude awakening next day!)

155 Croatia's coach Miroslav Blazevic claimed he knew his team would reach the 1998 finals because he'd been told as much by – who? (Clue: somebody who helped Blazevic seer what was coming, obviously.)

156 Following a half-time tactics talk during their group match against Germany in 1970, Morocco started the second half with – what? (Clue: a half-hearted performance.)

157 Successive England managers picked right back Viv Anderson for their squads in 1982 and 1986, using him to make runs up and down – where? (Clue: right back!)

158 As the team landed in USA for the 1994 finals, Brazil's coach Carlos Alberto Perreira told his 17-year-old star Ronaldo he was only there to – what? (Clue: take note, young man!)

159 When Bulgaria heard that in their 1998 group game against Nigeria they'd be up against a squad who, it was said, had brought their own witch doctors with them, they recruited – what? (Clue: it was a tactic "witch" didn't work.)

WHEEEEEEEEE!

160 To show that tactics play their part even when the game is over, when Brazil finished a bruising game against Hungary in 1954 they hurried off the pitch and waited for them – where? (Clue: it wasn't a tunnel of love.)

Answers:

149 Earrings – he also suggested they get their hair cut!

150 Brush his teeth – he'd borrowed some toothpaste from one of his players before the first game and did the same for every match afterwards. Maybe that's how his team brushed aside the opposition to win the trophy!

151 A smelly cheese made from sheep's milk. Maybe it helped their baaa-ll control!

152 School – in May, 1993, schoolboy Farooq was allowed two weeks off (making up for what he'd missed with homework!) to become the youngest World Cup player to date.

153 Being packed off to join the Italian army.

154 Partying – and staying up half the night before the game!

155 A fortune-teller (otherwise known as a seer, geddit?) – in the event, Croatia went on to achieve third place; maybe they'd have done even better if they'd been allowed to play their games with a crystal ball?

156 Half a team – the referee had started the second half without checking that all the Moroccans were back on the pitch!

157 The touchline ... but only the *outside* – although he did a lot of warming up, Anderson didn't actually get on to the pitch once in either tournament.

158 Learn – Perreira also added, "Your time will come later." Ronaldo must hope those words come true one day. Although he was in the team in 1998, Brazil lost in the final to France.

159 Three witches of their own – named Villi, Nadia and Mailina, they cast spells for Bulgaria to win. They didn't work: the game ended 1-0 to Nigeria.

160 The players' tunnel – the Brazilians turned out the lights in the tunnel, gave the Hungarians bunches of fives as they came off, then invaded their changing room to continue the fight!

WORLD CUP PLAYERS

To become a World Cup star you've got to start young. You don't need lots of flashy gear, either. Like lots of his countrymen, the famous Brazilian Pelé began playing barefooted in the street with a "ball" made out of rags.

Question:

161 Why did Pelé also spend part of this time playing in the pitch dark?

a) Because he wanted to learn how to control the ball with his eyes shut.

b) Because there were no lights in his street.

c) Because he used to sneak into a local ground after the floodlights were switched off.

Answer:

161 b) – and why was Pelé's street completely in the dark for a while? Because he'd busted the one street light it had with a misdirected shot!

Crazy careers

Appearing in the World Cup is the high spot of any player's career, the chance to show the world what it would have missed if they hadn't become footballers…

Match these World Cup stars to the jobs they might have ended up doing instead of playing football.

162 Lilian Thuram, winning wing-back with France in 1998, dreamed of becoming a what? (Hint: France blessed the fact that he didn't.)

Car mechanic

163 Vladimir Beara, Yugoslavia's 1958 goalkeeper, trained as a what? (Hint: he was light on his feet.)

Coal deliveryman

164 Geoff Hurst, England's 1966 hat-trick hero could have had a sporting career as a what? (Hint: he was all-white at another game!)

Member of Parliament

165 Gerd Müller, scorer of West Germany's winning goal in the 1974 final, used to be an apprentice what? (Hint: maybe it's why he was so good at threading the ball through narrow gaps.)

Athlete

166 Andreas Kopke, Germany's 1998 goalkeeper, is also a qualified what? (Hint: it could suggest he's a self-starter in the mornings!)

Priest

167 Eusebio, ace striker in the Portugal team that reached the 1966 semi-finals, used to act as a what? (Hint: he threw this job in once he'd started playing!)

Spy

168 Slaven Bilic, defender for Croatia in 1998, was studying to become a what? (Hint: he knows the rules.)

Watermelon salesman

169 The one and only Pelé of Brazil, a winner in 1958 and 1970 used to be an apprentice what? (Hint: he gave it up to put his best foot forward.)

Cricketer

170 Gordon Banks, goalkeeper in England's 1966 team, used to be a what? (Hint: he got the sack every day!)

Ballet Dancer

171 Alex Villaplane, captain of France in 1930, was found guilty of being a what? (Hint: he preferred to play for the opposition.)

Weaver

172 Gary Lineker, England's top-scoring striker in 1986 and 1990, was a champion schoolboy what? (Hint: it explains why he was a speedy player.)

Shoemaker

173 Ze Carlos, Brazilian full-back whose first-ever World Cup appearance was in the 1998 semi-final, used to be a what? (Hint: a tasty player!)

Lawyer

174 And finally, Josef Bozsik, of Hungary's 1954 beaten finalists, later became a what? (Hint: he argued – but not with the referee.)

Ball-boy

Answers:

162 e) – and he scored the two semi-final goals that gave his country a win over Croatia; they wouldn't have had a prayer otherwise!

163 i) – until he took his first steps towards becoming a footballer!

164 h) – he played first-class cricket for Essex.

165 j) – he gave up his apprenticeship to become a professional footballer and started weaving his way through the opposition.

166 a) – but then, as a goalkeeper, he already knew about ball bearings!

167 m) – he was a ball-boy at an exhibition match in Mozambique when he saw England's winger Stanley Matthews in action and decided he wanted to be a star like him.

168 l) – he was studying law at university while he was playing for Everton in the FA Premiership.

169 k) – he gave up his apprenticeship to play for top side Santos – aged 15!

170 b) – maybe that's why he had bags of talent!

171 f) – during World War Two, he helped the Nazis after they'd invaded France … until he was caught by the French Resistance and executed.

172 d) – he was Leicestershire Schools 400 metres champion.

173 g) – a late starter, who didn't reach top-level club football until he was 28.

174 c) – what's more, for over six years he combined this with being a footballer.

Odd couples

World Cup players have lots of things in common, of course: they're all great footballers, they're all representing their country, they're all hoping to win and so on.

But sometimes players have some quite peculiar things in common as well – like these odd couples...

What do these pairs of World Cup players have in common?

175 In the qualifiers for 1998, England's Paul Ince injured the same part of his body as Rajko Mitic of Yugoslavia had in 1950. What was it?

a) His knee.
b) His head.
c) His bum.

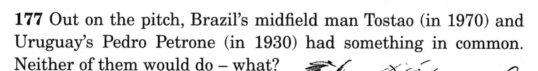

176 Croatia's Davor Suker (in 1998) and West Germany's Gerd Müller (in 1970) both ended the tournament being given flashy pairs of boots. What colour were they?

a) Gold.
b) Silver.
c) Bronze.

177 Out on the pitch, Brazil's midfield man Tostao (in 1970) and Uruguay's Pedro Petrone (in 1930) had something in common. Neither of them would do – what?

a) Take corners.
b) Make sliding tackles.
c) Head the ball.

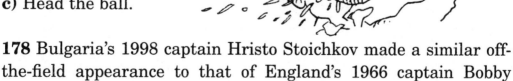

178 Bulgaria's 1998 captain Hristo Stoichkov made a similar off-the-field appearance to that of England's 1966 captain Bobby Moore. What was it?

| IN AN ADVENTURE FILM | IN A TOP-SECURITY PRISON | IN A RACING CAR |

179 Antonio Carbajal of Mexico and Germany's Lothar Matthaus both have an interest in the number five. Was it because each of them...

a) Wore the number five throughout their career.

b) Played in five World Cups.

c) Once scored five goals in a World Cup match.

180 Jack Charlton of England (in 1966) and Jimmy McIlroy of Northern Ireland (in 1982) were just two of many players who have been called on during World Cups to pass an odd test of accuracy. But accuracy at what?

a) Signing their name.

b) Peeing into a bottle.

c) Kicking a camera.

Answers:

175 b) – Ince cut his head during a match against Italy, went off to the dressing room to have the injury stitched – and found the room locked! The key was finally found and he returned to the match. The difference with Mitic was that he did it as he was leaving the changing room and had to be patched up before he could start the match.

176 a) They both ended as "golden boot" winners for being top scorer of the tournament.

177 c) – Tostao wouldn't because heading could have worsened a bad eye condition which later needed an operation to save his sight. Petrone didn't have a decent excuse: he simply wouldn't head the ball because he didn't want to mess up his hairstyle!

178 a) Moore appeared (along with Pelé and others) in a prisoner-of-war film called *Escape to Victory*. Stoichkov's star performance was in a Bulgarian mafia movie called *Spanish Fly*.

179 b) Carbajal was Mexico's goalkeeper from 1950 to 1966 … and won nothing. Matthaus played for Germany from 1982 to 1998, collecting a loser's medal in 1982 and, as captain, actually lifting the World Cup trophy in 1990.

180 b) – for drugs-testing. Charlton was picked so often to be tested that at the end of the 1966 tournament the testers gave him a trophy to remember them by! McIlroy wasn't quite so successful; he'd lost so much water during the match that he couldn't go until he'd been given large quantities of beer!

Tricky training

Training for the big games of the World Cup is essential. Teams take over complete hotels and set up large training camps with full-size pitches and plenty of space so that they can practise their skills and work out their tactics.

It wasn't always this way. In 1930, the French team arrived for the first World Cup to discover that they'd been given a training pitch that was only the size of a basketball court!

Question:

181 What else did it lack?

a) Goals.

b) Line markings.

c) Grass.

Answer:

181 a) – presumably they had to put down their jumpers!

IT WAS A GOAL!   IT HIT THE POST!

Question:

182 Nowadays teams are much better prepared in all areas of fitness. For the 1998 finals, the England squad employed Dr Jan Rougier as their very own "Doctor of the Body", one of whose jobs was to advise the players on – what?

a) How to chew their food.

b) How to cut their toenails.

c) How to check for nits.

Answer:
182 a) – food was his speciality; he advised the players on what to eat, when to eat and, yes, how to chew their food so that it was digested more quickly.

Here are some facts about other tricky World Cup training techniques. The sentences have been jumbled up, with the underlined words belonging to a different sentence. Sort them out to reveal the truth!

183 During the 1998 finals, the England players could have <u>an orange</u> on training days but not on match days.

184 Also in 1998, the USA's Frankie Hejduk carried out a vital part of his pre-match preparation in the changing room by turning his <u>slipper</u> back-to-front.

185 Training or not, 1970 Brazilian midfielder Gerson couldn't resist <u>baked beans</u>.

186 After getting injured during a match in 1990, England striker Gary Lineker had to wear his <u>wedding ring</u> during training.

187 Many of the Saudi Arabian players prepared for their 1998 matches by sleeping on <u>a World Cup football</u>.

188 The father of Brazil's 1958 defender Djalmar Santos insisted that the best training for his schoolboy son was a nightly dose of <u>superstition</u>.

189 When he was a youngster, Diego Maradona of Argentina trained by using <u>pictures</u>.

190 England's 1966 defender, Jack Charlton, always left some of his training until seconds before a match kicked off! This was because he liked to carry out a bit of last-minute <u>homework</u>.

191 Nery Pumpido, Argentina's goalkeeper, suffered a freak training accident in 1986 when he jumped up and got his <u>shorts</u> caught in one of the net-hooks behind the crossbar of his goal.

192 Part of Brazil's training in 1958 involved drawing <u>the floor</u>.

193 In 1998, spoon-bending exhibitionist Uri Geller tried to help out with England's training by sending all the players a copy of his *Little Book of Mind Power* each of which, he said, had been rubbed with <u>cigarettes</u>.

Answers:

183 baked beans – the thinking was that they were hard to digest and would give the players wind ... which wouldn't help them put the wind up the other side!

184 shorts – he thought it brought him luck. It didn't: the USA lost every game.

185 cigarettes – Gerson was a non-stop smoker (except on the pitch!).

186 slipper – his toe had swollen and he couldn't get his football boots on.

187 the floor – as staff at their hotel discovered when they found beds wheeled out into the corridors!

188 homework – after getting caught playing truant from school, Djalmar's dad stopped him playing football until he'd passed all his exams.

189 an orange – he juggled with one instead of a ball!

190 superstition – Charlton simply had to bang a practice ball into the net just before kick-off. In the 1966 World Cup final he lined up his shot – and missed! He had to frantically get hold of another one and bang that in before the game began.

191 wedding ring – Pumpido dislocated his finger. Fortunately for him it was possible to put it back into position. He went on to play in every game and "pick up" a winner's medal!

192 pictures – one of Brazil's backroom team was a doctor who got them to draw pictures of men. His theory was that a good team had a mix of brainy players (who drew detailed pictures) and thick players (who drew stick men!).

193 a World Cup football – the ball used in the 1966 World Cup final, to be exact. Geller also claimed to have put a special dose of energy on the World Cup trophy so that it would be attracted to England! If he did, then it suffered a power cut: the thing didn't make it out of France.

The name game

Names must be important, otherwise why would players have them written all over the backs of their shirts?

Some World Cup players, though, have had names they'd have preferred not to advertise. Like…

● The forward who played in Cameroon's 1998 qualifying matches and would definitely have been a clear winner of any worst-name-for-a-striker award: Jean-Jacques Misse-Misse.

● In 1938, the Egyptian goalkeeper simply must have got the hump about the number of jokes made about his name: Moustafa Kamel.

● And then there was the perfectly named South African who was sent home after misbehaving himself at the 1998 finals: Naughty Mokoena.

Question:

194 Then there was the referee at the 1954 finals. What was his name?

a) Clueless.

b) Pitiless.

c) Faultless.

Answer:
194 c) – and he soon showed the players the errors of their ways!

Fans seems to like calling players names – even those players they support. Giving them nicknames is a favourite pastime on the terraces. Match this batch of nicknames with their owners…

195 Louis Airton Barroso Olivera was born in Brazil but went to live in Belgium when he was 15, which is how he came to be a member of their 1998 squad. As his name was a bit of a mouthful, his team-mates called him…

196 In 1938 another Brazilian, Leonidas, was so famous for his spectacular overhead kicks he was called…

197 Russia's star goalkeeper from 1954 to 1966, Lev Yashin, didn't think it was a bit fishy when people called him…

198 The nicknames of two cool strikers in 1998, Italy's Christian Vieri and Holland's Dennis Bergkamp, have a word in common. It is…

199 To fans at his French club, Marseille, England's 1990 winger Chris Waddle was known as "The…"

200 Because he looked clumsy, a big-headed TV commentator once called Poland's 1974 goalkeeper Jan Tomaszewski a…

201 Everybody called Garrincha of Brazil "you little…"

202 Finally, a twosome. Just Fontaine and Raymond Kopa, of France's 1958 team, played so well together they were known as "The…"

Answers:

195 Lulu – which hopefully didn't suggest he played like a big girl's blouse!

196 Rubber Man.

197 Octopus.

198 Ice – Vieri is known as "the ice giant", Bergkamp as "the ice man" (so do they call the fortunes they earn "ice lolly"?).

199 Crazy Dribbler – maybe they'd seen him eating an ice-lolly!

200 Clown – the big head was manager and pundit Brian Clough, when commentating on the vital qualifying match between England and Poland which England had to win to qualify. Tomaszewski had the last laugh, though – he kept England out, Poland qualified, and went on to take third place in the 1974 finals.

201 Bird – because of the way he used to fly down the wing!

202 Tandem Terrible – it's French, of course, and means "terrible twosome".

Injury time

What with World Cup finals taking nearly a month to complete, it's no surprise that many players have call for pills, potions or other remedies to sort them out.

Here are some misfortunes that players have suffered to various parts of their bodies during World Cup competitions. Unfortunately, because the editor is a bit squeamish, the body parts have been jumbled up. Unscramble them.

203 In 1962, England defender Peter Swan had a running problem. This badly affected his MOTHSAC.

204 Injured during the 1970 semi-final against Italy,

West Germany's captain Franz Beckenbauer had to play a large part of the game with his RUDE HOLS in a sling.

205 In 1986, Trevor Steven of England simply couldn't bring himself to talk about his HOT TAR...

206 ...well, not until it was cured by giving him an injection in the CADS BIKE.

207 In 1970, England's Bobby Charlton needed plenty of cream rubbed on his badly sunburned PADS BLOT.

208 Finally, to a whole team who weren't ill, but just looked off-colour – because they'd treated themselves and ended up with A WIRY HELLO.

Answers:

203 STOMACH – he'd contracted a very dangerous disease called dysentery, which caused him to do a lot of running ... to the loo!

204 SHOULDER – he'd dislocated it, but as West Germany had used all their substitutes he had to play on.

205 THROAT – Trevor Steven had caught tonsillitis...

206 ...and **BACKSIDE** – because that's where the doctor thought it would be most effective to get him "up and about" quickly!

I THINK I NEED THE LOO!

207 BALD SPOT – because Charlton was quite bald.

208 YELLOW HAIR – to celebrate reaching the second round, all the Romanian outfield players bleached their hair the same colour.

Are you talking about me?

One of the tricky things about being a top player is that everybody has got something to say about you. It can be something nice, something nasty … or something unprintable!

Who was being talked about in this selection of quotes about World Cup players? Match the quote with the player.

209 "He is far too handsome to be a footballer. I don't know whether to kick him or kiss him," said Argentina's Juan Veron, in 1998.

210 "He is the peerless goalkeeper of the century," said Portugal's Eusebio of this Russian.

211 "Even his feet are intelligent," said Michel Hidalgo, France's manager in 1982.

212 "He was an extraordinary player – the others used to give the ball to him when they wanted a rest," said Leonel Sanchez (Chile, 1962) about this South American opponent.

Très brainy, Michel Platini.

England's buzzing winger, Steve Coppell.

Argentina's star, Diego Maradona.

England's model captain, David Beckham.

213 "Get away little fly," said West Germany's giant defender Hans-Peter Briegel, when tackled by this player during a match in the 1982 finals.

214 "They are fielding him and ten robots," said the former Brazilian star Pelé, of one West German player and his team-mates in the 1982 World Cup.

215 "With him even Arsenal would have won the World Cup," said England manager Bobby Robson, on one man's peformances in the 1986 finals.

216 "It was like an ostrich trying to stamp on an eel," said Newspaper reports of the USA versus Brazil match in 1994. They weren't being too complimentary about the success of this USA defender in marking Brazil's nippy forward, Romario.

217 "That goal and his big green eyes conquered me!" said popstar Madonna, showing us she knew what was important about football after watching this player score for Italy in 1990.

"Levitating" Lev Yashin of Russia.

Good "looking" Roberto Baggio.

Brazil's wicked winger Garrincha, a player who never put his feet up!

Karl-Heinz Rummenigge, even though he was a goal scoring machine!

Non-flying centre-back Alexi Lalas.

Answers:
209 David Beckham

210 Lev Yashin
211 Michel Platini
212 Garrincha

213 Steve Coppell
214 Karl-Heinz Rummenigge
215 Diego Maradona (Tottenham fans may disagree)
216 Alexi Lalas
217 Roberto Baggio

WICKED WORLD CUP MATCHES

Matches in the World Cup are often so exciting you simply don't know what's going to happen next – although in France in 1998 there was one very different match: one in which nobody knew what was going to happen *before* the game began!

An hour before the group match between Norway and Brazil, out on to the pitch in front of 60,000 spectators came two men dressed in black … and a girl wearing white.

Question:
218 What happened next?
a) One of the men married the girl.
b) One of the men married the girl *and* the other man.

Answer:
218 a) and **b)** as the girl was Brazilian and one of the men, her husband-to-be, was Norwegian, they'd persuaded the authorities to let them get married on the pitch before the game began. The second man in black was the priest who married them by conducting the wedding ceremony!

Mad matches

Here are some famously mad incidents from World Cup matches. In each case, what happened next?

219 In the 1930 semi-final between Argentina and the USA, the USA's angry medical assistant threw his bag on the ground and…
a) Started crying.
b) Fainted.
c) Punctured the ball.

220 In the 1938 semi-final, no sooner had Italy's captain Guiseppe Meazza converted a penalty against Brazil than...

HIS SHORTS FELL DOWN | AN EXCITED FAN RAN ON AND KISSED HIM | THE REFEREE WAS BITTEN BY A DOG

221 After hitting an equalizer in their 1954 semi-final against Hungary, Juan Hohberg of Uruguay was...
a) Carried shoulder-high round the pitch.
b) Carried back to the centre-circle.
c) Carried off.

222 Unhappy after conceding a goal to Mexico in their 1970 group match, the El Salvador team refused to...
a) Speak to the referee.
b) Kick-off.
c) Come out for the second half.

223 In the opening game of the 1994 finals, substitute Marco Etcheverry of Bolivia finally got his chance, running on to join the match against Germany in the 78th minute – and became...
a) The first substitute to score with his first touch.
b) The first player to be carried off without even touching the ball.
c) The first player to be sent off in the opening game of the finals.

224 Objecting to a goal scored by France in 1982, because they'd stopped playing after hearing a whistle from the crowd, Kuwait were ready to walk off the pitch until they were talked out of it by...
a) An official.
b) A prince.
c) A supporter.

225 An earlier French team, back in 1930, were sweeping on to the attack with six minutes of their match against Argentina left to play when...
a) The referee accidentally blew for full-time.
b) The Argentine fans invaded the pitch.
c) The ball burst.

226 In 1962 the Italian newspapers printed nasty things about their next opponents and host country Chile. In particular they said that Chilean girls were ugly! To apologize, when the Italian players ran out on to the pitch before the game they were carrying...

a) Chocolates.
b) Flowers.
c) Plates of pizza.

Answers:
219 b) – in his bag a bottle of an anaesthetic called chloroform had broken and he was overcome by the fumes!

220 a) – they'd been ripped in an earlier incident but he waited until he'd made "short" work of the penalty before changing them!

221 c) – he was knocked out by his own team-mates in the goal celebrations!

BOY! THEY REALLY KNOW HOW TO CELEBRATE A GOAL!

222 b) – the referee solved the problem by blowing for half-time.

223 c) – he'd been on the pitch for just four minutes.

224 a) and b) ... and probably **c)** as well – the persuading was done by Prince Fahid, who was also President of the Kuwait Football Association.

225 a) – and then the Argentine fans invaded the pitch! The game was restarted once it had been cleared and the final six minutes played.

226 b) – they were booed, lost 0-2 and had two men sent off. You could say the game turned ugly!

Oh, referee!

Referees can never win.

Whatever decision they make, one side or the other will think it's a monstrous mistake. That was certainly the case in the 1934 World Cup qualifying match between Hungary and Bulgaria ... because it was refereed by a certain Herr Frankenstein!

DO YOU HAVE A PROBLEM WITH MY DECISION?

NO! IT WAS A MONSTER DECISION

How good is your decision-making about decision-making? Here's a quiz about decisions made by referees involved with World Cup games. Match the incident with the decision.

227 ONE TEAM ARE ABOUT TO SCORE BUT YOU...

228 THE FOOTBALL SUPPLIED BY THE HOST COUNTRY IS USELESS SO YOU...

229 DRIVING HOME AFTER A CONTROVERSIAL MATCH YOU STOP AT A SET OF TRAFFIC LIGHTS WHICH INSPIRE YOU TO...

230 YOUR WATCH SAYS THERE'S SOME INJURY-TIME LEFT TO PLAY BUT YOU...

231 YOU'VE JUST AWARDED A FREE-KICK SO YOU...

232 A PLAYER HAS BEEN MOANING AT YOU ALL GAME SO YOU...

233 A FORWARD PUNCHES THE BALL INTO THE NET BUT YOU...

(a) STAND WHERE THE BALL IS LIKELY TO HIT YOU.

(b) DISALLOW A FAIR GOAL TO SHOW HIM WHO'S BOSS.

(c) SWAP IT WHILE NOBODY'S LOOKING.

(d) GIVE A GOAL.

(e) BLOW FOR FULL-TIME ANYWAY.

(f) INVENT RED AND YELLOW CARDS.

(g) BLOW FOR FULL-TIME AND DISALLOW THE GOAL.

Answers:

227 g) – Sweden and Brazil were drawing 1-1 when Brazil took a corner … only to discover that referee Clive Thomas had blown for full-time while the ball was in the air.

228 c) – this happened during games in Chile in 1962; so as not to offend the hosts, referees would switch their poor-quality ball for a decent one the first chance they got.

229 f) – Ken Aston was actually an ex-referee. He was acting as a FIFA official when England played Argentina in 1966 and the Argentine captain refused to leave the pitch, claiming that he didn't know he'd been sent off because the referee didn't speak his language. The traffic lights gave him the idea of recommending to FIFA that referees carry red and yellow cards to make their decisions clear to everybody. They were used for the first time in 1970.

230 e) – it was claimed that in 1986 referees were encouraged not to add on too much time because it would save TV companies money on satellite hire.

231 a) – after awarding a free kick to England against Argentina in 1986, where did the referee stand? At the end of the defensive wall, where John Barnes' kick found him!

232 b) – Italy's Benito Lorenzi had been moaning at the referee throughout the group game against Switzerland in 1954. When he had what looked like a perfectly good goal ruled out it was generally thought to be a case of ref's revenge!

233 d) – in his first (and last) World Cup game, Tunisian referee Ali Bennaceur didn't see Argentina's Diego Maradona punch the ball into the net against England in 1986.

Seeing red

The foul footballers of the World Cup have seen their fair share of red cards, though few as quickly as José Batista of Argentina. He was sent off in the very first minute of the 1986 group game against Scotland!

Here are some red card riddles. But are they true or false?

234 Frank Rijkaard of Holland was sent off against West Germany in 1990 because he punched German forward Rudi Voeller in the face. **True or false?**

235 In 1994, Germany's Stefan Effenberg was sent off for making rude signs at the crowd. **True or false?**

236 After Brazil's Garrincha was sent off against Chile in 1962 he was hit by a toilet roll. **True or false?**

237 During the Brazil v Hungary game in 1954, Brazil's Humberto Tozzi was sent off even though he went down on his knees and begged for mercy. **True or false?**

238 In the 1966 quarter-final between England and Argentina, the referee sent off Argentina's captain Antonio Rattin because, he said, Rattin had a really nasty look on his face. **True or false?**

239 Czechoslovakia's Lubomir Moravcik found himself leaving the field against West Germany in 1990 because he'd kicked his own boot in the air. **True or false?**

240 N'Daye of Zaire was finally sent off against Yugoslavia in 1974 after committing no less than 15 bad fouls. **True or false?**

241 England's Ray Wilkins was shown the red card in 1986 because he'd made an angry pass. **True or false?**

242 When the idea of referee's coloured cards was introduced in the 1970 World Cup, they were only given yellow cards. **True or false?**

Answers:

234 False – he spat in his face. Voeller wasn't allowed to carry on dribbling, though – he was also sent off, for what he'd said to Rijkaard.

235 False – but he was sent off after a fashion ... sent off home, by Germany's management team.

236 False – he was hit by a bottle (thrown from the crowd, not by the ref!).

237 True – yes, the referee still sent the beggar off!

238 True – Rattin was sent off for foul body language!

239 True – it happened after Moravcik's claim for a penalty was turned down. The referee decided this was dissent and gave him his second yellow card.

240 False – he'd actually done nothing wrong at all. It was a case of mistaken identity and the referee had sent off the wrong person. The real culprit was N'Daye's teammate, Mwepu.

241 True – the angry pass was to the referee – he threw the ball at him! Some nasty people suggested it was the most accurate pass Wilkins had played all game!

242 False – as now, they had both red and yellow cards in their pockets – it was just that none of them pulled out the red. Amazingly, during the 1970 finals not a single player was sent off!

GREAT GOALS

What the fans want at the World Cup is plenty of goals – so long as they're scored at the right end, that is.

England's supporters found this out in 1954, when defender Jimmy Dickinson scored the only goal of his international career in the group match against Belgium – an own goal!

The feelings of Scotland's fans were bruised even more that same year. Crowding round their TV sets to watch their team meet Uruguay in the first-ever live football match broadcast in Scotland, they saw no less than seven goals. Unfortunately, all seven whizzed into the Scottish net!

Question:

243 Some World Cup goalscorers are lucky enough to gain even more than the thrill of seeing the ball hit the back of the net. When Khalid Mubarak scored for the United Arab Emirates against West Germany in 1990, what did he pick up as a bonus from the government of his country?

a) A Rolls Royce car.
b) A house.
c) A small oil well.

Answer:
243 a) – not bad considering his team were beaten 5-1!

Going for goals

Here are some questions about World Cup goals. How well can you score?

244 In qualifying for the 1998 finals Iran really built up a head of steam, beating The Maldives 17-0 in one match – with ten of the goals coming in the same way. How?
a) Penalties.
b) Headers.
c) Corners.

245 Raimondo Orsi scored a spectacular goal to help win the World Cup for Italy in 1934 by pretending to what?
a) Head the ball … before launching into an overhead kick.
b) Run away … before turning round and scoring with a diving header.
c) Shoot with his left foot … before hitting it with his right foot.

246 Jose Chilavert, goalkeeper in Paraguay's 1998 squad, managed to score what?
a) A spectacular World Cup goal for Paraguay.
b) Two own goals in one match.
c) An own goal and saved a penalty in the same match.

247 England's great goalscorer, Bobby Charlton, seeing the ball rocketing goalwards against Mexico in 1966, memorably let rip with a very loud World Cup what?
a) Shout of joy.
b) Cry of pain.
c) Howl of terror.

248 A single goal caused a lot of controversy in 1982. After West Germany had beaten Austria 1-0 they were accused of what?
a) Dirty play.
b) Picking on the referee.
c) Not trying.

249 Rene Higuita of Columbia once gave away a terrible World Cup goal. How?
a) Trying a "scorpion kick" clearance that didn't work.
b) Losing the ball while dribbling it.
c) Conceding a penalty for pulling an attacker down by his shorts.

Answers:
244 b) – The Maldives are tiny islands and their players were much the same, being about 15cm (6 inches) shorter than their opponents – which is why the Iranians kept the ball in the air!
245 c) – it was such a spectacular goal that newspaper photographers who'd missed it asked Orsi to do it again the next day. He tried time and again – but couldn't do it!
246 a) – Chilavert charged out from his goal to score for his team in a qualifying match against Argentina which ended 1-1.

247 a) – Charlton shouted, "She's there!" as he scored with a thunderbolt for England's first goal of the finals against Mexico in 1966.

248 c) – West Germany and Austria knew that a 1-0 result would put both teams into the next round – so *neither* of them tried!

249 b) – in extra-time against Cameroon in 1990, Higuita lost the ball while trying to dribble it near the halfway line!

Penalty pains

Nowadays, as England's fans know only too well, penalty shoot-outs can be a painful part of the World Cup finals.

Not every player dislikes them, though. In 1990, David O'Leary of the Republic of Ireland came on for his first appearance of the tournament in extra-time against Romania in a second-round match and ended up scoring the winner in the penalty shoot-out.

Here are some statements about momentous World Cup penalties and penalty shoot-outs. Are they true or false?

250 The first-ever penalty was awarded in the 1978 World Cup final between Holland and West Germany. **True or false?**

251 ...it was awarded in the first minute. **True or false?**

252 Goalkeeper Sepp Maier was the first West German player to touch the ball in the match when he tipped the kick round the post. **True or false?**

253 The second-ever penalty kick in a World Cup final was awarded four years later, in 1982. **True or false?**

254 England were the first country to lose a match in the finals on a penalty shoot-out. **True or false?**

255 The first player to miss a penalty in a shoot-out was England's Stuart Pearce. **True or false?**

256 Italy were defeated on penalties in 1990, 1994 and 1998. **True or false?**

257 In the 1990 finals, both semi-finals were decided on penalties. **True or false?**

258 In 1986, two out of the four quarter-finals were decided on penalties. **True or false?**

259 France only became the 1998 World Cup winners by surviving two penalty shoot-outs, in the second round and the quarter-final. **True or false?**

Answers:
250 True – and English referee Jack Taylor was the man with the whistle!
251 True.

252 False – Holland's Johann Neeskens scored. Maier *was* the first West German player to touch the ball, but only when he picked it out of the net!

253 False – it was awarded 25 minutes later (and Paul Breitner of West Germany scored it to put them level and on the way to a 2-1 win).

254 False – it was France, in 1982.

255 False – that honour, during a 1982 semi-final, fell to Uli Stielike – a German!

256 True – by Argentina in the semi-final in 1990, Brazil (in the final) in 1994, and by France in the 1998 quarter-final.

257 True – West Germany beat England and Argentina beat Italy.

258 False – it was even worse, with three out of the four quarter-finals being decided on a shoot-out.

259 False – they beat Italy in a shoot-out, but managed to beat Paraguay in the second round by scoring the first-ever World Cup "golden goal" to finish the match in extra-time.

Golden boots

A special award is given at the end of the World Cup finals – not to a team but to a player. It's a pair of golden boots.

Question:

260 How does a player win them?

a) By being voted the Player of the Tournament by the other players.

b) By finishing as top scorer.

c) By captaining the winning team in the final.

Answer:

260 b) the Golden Boot Award is for the top scorer in the World Cup finals. (They're not as valuable as they sound, though: the boots aren't actually made of solid gold, just designed to look as though they are.)

Question:

261 In 1962, six players finished the competition with four goals each:

Albert (Hungary), Garrincha (Brazil), Ivanov (USSR), Jerkovic (Yugoslavia), Sanchez (Chile) and Vavà (Brazil). Who won the Golden Boot award?

a) The players shared it.

b) The winner was drawn out of a bag.

c) Nobody.

Twinkling toes

Golden Boot winners usually have a tale to tell. Here's a quiz about some of them. Work out which tale belongs to which of these twinkling-toed Golden Boot winners:

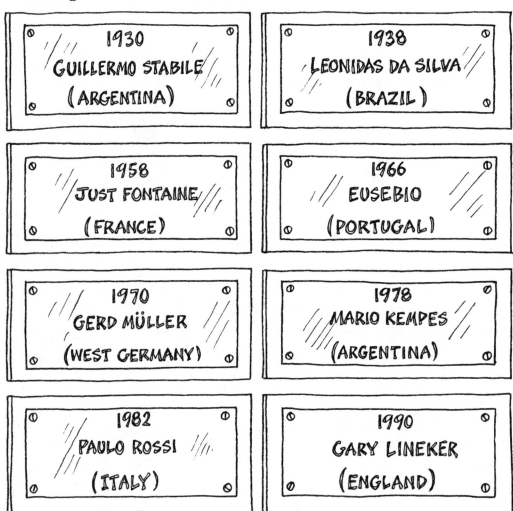

1930
GUILLERMO STABILE
(ARGENTINA)

1938
LEONIDAS DA SILVA
(BRAZIL)

1958
JUST FONTAINE
(FRANCE)

1966
EUSEBIO
(PORTUGAL)

1970
GERD MÜLLER
(WEST GERMANY)

1978
MARIO KEMPES
(ARGENTINA)

1982
PAULO ROSSI
(ITALY)

1990
GARY LINEKER
(ENGLAND)

262 As a reward for winning the Golden Boot he was offered 1,000 bottles of wine and Italian-made shoes for life!

263 This Golden Boot winner didn't expect to be picked. Then, in training, the first-choice striker, René Bliard, injured himself kicking the ground instead of the ball and he got his chance. His total of 13 goals in six games is still a record.

264 His six goals won him the Golden Boot outright; not bad given that his team, England, were knocked out in the quarter-finals!

265 Having a shave made all the difference for this man! He'd grown a gaucho-style moustache for the finals, but when he still hadn't found the net after the first three games his team-mates talked him into shaving it off ... and he promptly scored six goals in the next four games as his country went on to win the trophy.

266 He scored nine goals in 1966, one of them in the 82nd minute of the semi-final against England which his team lost, leaving him in tears.

267 He missed the first game of the finals, only getting his chance when team-mate Manuel Ferreira went off to take a university exam. What happened? He scored a hat trick, kept his place and finished with eight goals in four matches!

268 His total was ten goals in six games, partly through the tactic he had with his captain of turning and shooting if he was passed the ball firmly. It might have been more but for the other part of the plan – if his captain passed the ball gently, then he had to give it back again and let his captain have a shot!

269 After winning the Golden Boot with seven goals he used his fame to sell cigars to his millions of fans by allowing his face to be shown on every packet.

HE'S MAKING A PACKET!

Answers:

262 Paulo Rossi (Italy).

263 Just Fontaine (France).

264 Gary Lineker (England).

265 Mario Kempes (Argentina).

266 Eusebio (Portugal).

267 Guillermo Stabile (Argentina).

268 Gerd Müller (West Germany) … and his captain was Franz Beckenbauer.

269 Leonidas da Silva (Brazil).

Final time

Time is very important, and never more so than in a World Cup final. Players wonder whether they'll be in the line-up at kick-off time; coaches wonder about what to say to their teams at half-time; the referee wonders when to blow the whistle for full-time; if it's needed, everybody wonders what will happen in extra-time – and maybe even after that...

Question:

270 If the 1970 final between Brazil and Italy had been a draw after extra-time, there would have been a replay. If that had ended in a draw after extra-time there would have been – what?
a) A second replay.
b) A penalty shoot-out.
c) A toss-up.

> **Answer:**
> **270 c)** – yes, in the days before penalty shoot-outs the World Cup winners really might have been decided by the toss of a coin!

Beginning, middle or end?

Time to try these questions about World Cup finals! Fill in each blank with either kick-off, half or full. There's no hurry, though. Take as much time as you need...

271 Much to the disappointment of football fans everywhere, Brazil's star forward Ronaldo was substituted in their 1998 World Cup final team before BLANK time.
272 In 1962 the referee for the Brazil versus Czechoslovakia final couldn't find the ball at BLANK time.

273 The ball had also disappeared in 1930, when Argentina and Uruguay met in the final at BLANK time.

274 A corner post problem at the 1974 final between West Germany and Holland caused a delay to BLANK time.

275 The 1950 World Cup final didn't have a BLANK time.

276 In 1938, when Italy beat Hungary, the Italians were relaxed and cruising well before BLANK time.

277 Alessandro Altobelli hit a goal for Italy against West Germany in the 1982 final. Strangely, he wasn't on the field at BLANK time or BLANK time.

Answers:

271 Kick-off – Ronaldo had been rushed to hospital with a mystery illness and had been replaced when the first Brazil team sheet that was announced. He recovered in time to substitute his substitute and start the match.

272 Full – the referee is supposed to leave the pitch with the ball … but this one had been stolen by Brazil's trainer, Americo, who refused to hand it over!

ONE, THAT'S ALL I WANT!

273 Half – both teams wanted to use their own ball for the match, so they played one half with each.

274 Kick-off – the problem being that the corner posts were missing!

275 Kick-off, half- or full-time – because there wasn't a World Cup final in 1950! The winners of the four first-round groups played a league competition, with the league champions taking the World Cup. It was pure luck the final league match between Uruguay and Brazil worked out to be the decider, with Uruguay needing to win the game to go top of the league – which they did.

276 Kick-off – after getting changed at their hotel the Italians got to the ground too early, so off they went for a little sight-seeing coach tour round Paris!

277 Kick-off AND full-time – Altobelli came on as a substitute in the sixth minute only to be substituted himself in the 88th minute ... but not before he'd banged in Italy's third goal in the 80th minute.

It's nearly all over – World Cup 1966

If you're English and you've got a relative or (worse!) a teacher who's over 40 years old, they'll almost certainly be happy to bore you stiff with their memories of how England won the World Cup in 1966.

So here's your chance to test them (or find out how much you've remembered, or maybe just to discover a fact or two you can use to bore them back) about what happened that year!

Here is a collection of World Cup facts. Do they apply to the magic year of 1966 – or to another year?

278 England warmed up for the finals by beating West Germany in a match at Wembley. **1966 or not?**

279 A fan could buy a season ticket to watch ten matches – including the World Cup final itself – for under £4. **1966 or not?**

280 The scorer of a last-minute goal later said that at the time he'd have been happy if his shot had sailed into the car park. **1966 or not?**

281 England manager Alf Ramsey substituted star midfield man Bobby Charlton in one match. **1966 or not?**

282 Stuart Pearce missed a penalty in one match. **1966 or not?**

283 The England captain, Bobby Moore, wiped his hands before greeting a VIP. **1966 or not?**

284 England met Argentina in the quarter-final and the result was 2-1. **1966 or not?**

285 France and Kuwait were in England's first-round group. **1966 or not?**

286 The host country team was jeered off the pitch after drawing 0-0 in their opening game. **1966 or not?**

287 England stars Bobby Charlton and Geoff Hurst become Sir Bobby and Sir Geoff. **1966 or not?**

Answers:

278 Yes, 1966 – the two teams met in February, with England winning 1-0.

279 Yes, 1966 – which is why the crowd at Wembley included a certain Michael Coleman and 99,999 other fans!

280 Yes, 1966 – it's what Geoff Hurst said about his famous third goal.

281 No, 1970 – in the quarter-final against Germany.

282 No, 1990 – in the semi-final penalty shoot-out, against Germany again.

283 Yes, 1966 – he did it just before receiving the World Cup from the Queen … wiping them on the velvet cloth at the front of the Royal Box!

284 No, 1986 – England beat Argentina 1-0 in the 1966 quarter-final.

> **285 No, 1982** – although France were in England's group in 1966, along with Mexico and Uruguay.
>
> **286 Yes, 1966** – England the hosts were booed off after their match against Uruguay!
>
> **287 No** – Charlton was knighted in 1994 and Hurst in 1998.

The quotes quiz

Let's leave the last word of this quiz book to a quiz about words which are set to last – quips and quotes about the World Cup that will live on wherever foul football is played. For instance, what were the wise words uttered by England manager Bobby Robson after guiding his team to the semi-finals in 1990?

Question:

288 Here are those words, but they've been scrambled. Arrange them into the correct order!

> **Answer:**
>
> **288** *We've got here but I don't know how.* He didn't have to wonder any further. England lost to Germany in a penalty shoot-out.

Every word counts

These World Cup quotes are as confused as some of their speakers. They're each missing a vital word. Put the following list of words in their rightful positions to produce the correct quotes.

amused, here, knotted, important, sitting, watch, Donald Duck, football, easy, ridiculous, control, work

289 A typical description of the state of play from USA commentators in 1994 whenever two sides were level: *The teams are BLANK at 1-1.*

290 Head of the Iran FA, Ali Asghar Manoussi, to his team during their 1998 qualifying games against The Maldives: *Take it BLANK.*

291 Proving that English commentators have a way with words, the BBC's John Motson said at the start of one match in the 1994 finals: *There are eleven men BLANK on yellow cards and that is a very uncomfortable position to be in.*

292 HRH Queen Elizabeth II is as entitled as any fan to voice her views. When England's Sol Campbell had a goal disallowed by the referee during the 1998 match against Argentina, Her Majesty said: *One is not BLANK at that!*

293 Alan Scott, Secretary of the Dog Owners' Association, after England manager Alf Ramsey had called the Argentinian players "animals" after a violent quarter-final: *This description is most unfair to our many members and their pets who insist on BLANK at all times.*

294 A press report after England were surprisingly beaten by the USA in 1950: *England were beaten by the Mickey Mouse and BLANK team.*

295 England player Wilf Mannion after this defeat: *BLANK! Can't we play them again?*

296 A bitter joke going the rounds in Glasgow when Scotland were knocked out of the 1978 finals after their manager Ally McLeod had predicted great things for them: *Mickey Mouse is going around wearing an Ally McLeod BLANK!*

297 Xavier Clemente, coach of Spain in 1998, felt that he didn't have many friends either, especially amongst newspaper reporters. He told them at one press conference: *There are a lot of people who know nothing about football and most of them are sitting BLANK.*

298 French defender Maxime Bossis after being on the losing side in two semi-finals, in 1982 and 1986, both to West Germany, shrugged: *Football is ridiculous, but life is BLANK too.*

299 Life came to a halt when Brazil played England in their 1970 group match. On the day of the match every street corner in Guadalajara, the Mexican city where the match was staged, carried posters proclaiming: *No BLANK today, we are off to see Pelé!*

300 Referees get talked about too. World Cup 1998 referee Paul Durkin complimented Scotland's Gary McAllister for a great pass during a match only to have the player reply: *What do you know about BLANK?*

Answers:

289 knotted – which means "tied", of course.

290 easy – they'd beaten The Maldives 17-0 and Manoussi was worried that the Iranian fans would expect them to score that many every game!

291 sitting

292 amused

293 control

294 Donald Duck

295 Ridiculous

296 watch

297 here

298 important

299 work – England's manager, Sir Alf Ramsey, had moaned about the Mexican fans so they were all supporting Brazil!

300 football

Final score

Bobby Robson may not have known how his team had succeeded but do you know how well you've done?

Over 250   World class performance!

150–249   Great stuff. Definitely a Golden Boot candidate.

50–149   Not bad. You could be a challenger in four years' time.

0–49   Sure you're not following the Rugby World Cup?